String Art

Basic steps to make String Art Designs

By

JAK

Acknowledgement

There are a lot of people to Thank who made this happen. It was very difficult to accomplish this task and all of them helped and supported me to make this happen. Very much thanks to everyone for your help and support.

Contents

Introduction

String art is basically "connecting two points with a string", as simple as that. String art is one of the most satisfying art in the world. The main attractiveness of this art is, you don't need high level training or knowledge to start doing it which makes it very easy. The result of this is very satisfying even if it is a simple task to complete a string art design. Anyone at any age can start doing string art.

The String Art patterns like String Art geometric patterns can be in any shape. Some examples are: String Art Circle Pattern, String Art triangle pattern, String Art Rectangle Pattern, String Art Square Pattern, String Art Star Pattern, String Art Pentagon pattern, String Art Hexagon Pattern, String Art Octagon Pattern.

The String Art designs can be used for various decorations, some of them are mentioned here:
String Art designs for Table decorations, String Art designs for Room decorations, String Art designs for Wall decorations, String Art designs for Stage decorations, String Art designs for Marriage decorations, String Art designs for Auditorium decorations

The String Art ideas can be implemented anywhere. Some of them are mentioned below:
String Art on Canvas, String Art designs on paper, String Art designs on wood, String Art on cardboard, String Art on wall, and String art on thermocol.

I have started and completed some string art designs and it helped me to relax and entertain myself. After creating some designs it became my hobby. It is one of the very satisfying art which anyone can start. I decided to make this book to share my experience and knowledge with everyone who is reading this book. I'm sure that some of you will get the same experience when doing string art.

Materials and tools used for string art

There are a lot of tools we can use to make string art. But I'm going to tell you the most basic tools and materials you can use to create simple string art.

String art platform: This can be a wooden board, Canvas, paper, cardboard, wall, thermocol, etc.

String: String can be any colour and size according to the platform size. But make sure that you have enough string length to complete one round of string art, because you should not join another string which will not give a perfect style.

Paper: To draw the outline of the design. You can draw the design outline in a paper and attach the paper to the wooden board to place the nails on the exact position.

Pencil, Ruler, Compass, Protractor: Used to draw the design either in a paper or directly to the wooden board or any other string art platform.

Hammer and Nails: To tie the string and make string art. You need to carefully place each nail in the exact position in the design to get perfect result. Choose the Hammer size and nail size according to the string art platform.

Scissors: To cut the string.

These are the basic tools and materials you need to start doing string art.

String Art Design: 1

Basic pattern: Triangle string Art

We are going to make the first basic String art as show in the below figure:

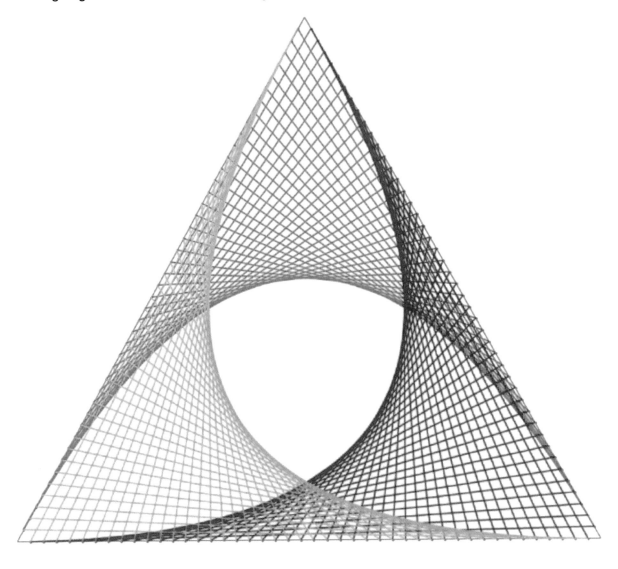

Materials used:

- Pencil and ruler
- Compass
- 3 different colour strings (Red, Green and Yellow). You can pick your own colors.
- Wooden board or Cardboard. You can pick your own platform like paper, thermocol, etc.
- Hammer and Nails (for wooden board).

Please follow the steps mentioned below to get a good result:

1. Draw a triangle with equal sides (Equilateral triangle). Length of the side should be according to the platform size.

For example: sides can be 20 cm if the platform size is 30cm (square shape). Draw the triangle with the sides of **AB=AC=BC=**20 cm. See the steps below to draw the equilateral triangle with 20cm side length.

1.1. Draw a line **AB** of 20cm using a pencil and ruler.

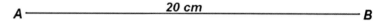

1.2. Take 20cm in the compass and mark arcs as shown in the figure from both points **A** and **B**.

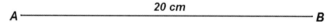

1.3. Draw lines from points **A** and **B** to the arc intersecting point **C**.

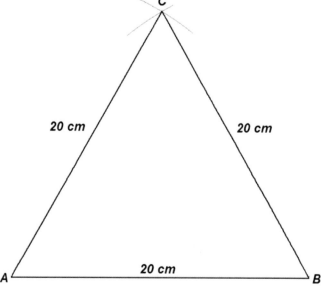

1.4. Now you have a triangle with 20cm each side.

2. Divide the sides of the triangle as shown in the figure. Take the number of dividing points according to the length of the side.

For example: distance between the points **A1** to **A2** can be 3 mm to 1cm.

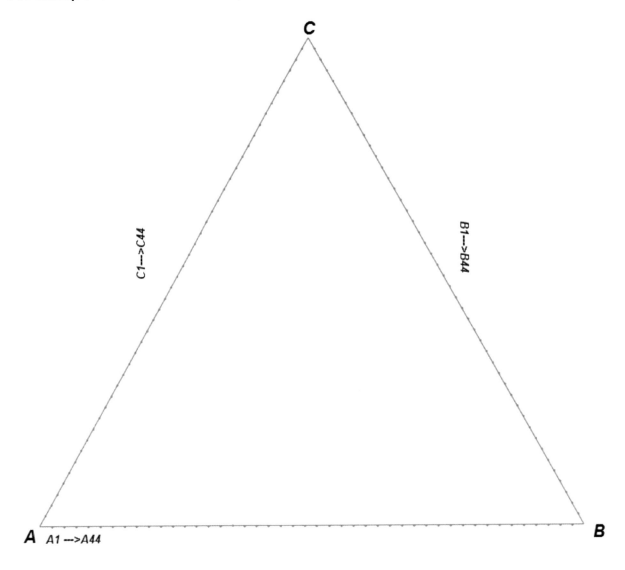

I have divided the side of the triangle into 44 points (**A1** to **A44**). You can decide the number of points you need on each side of the triangle. The perfect ratio will give a good result. But if you are a beginner then it will be easy if you take less number of dividing points (distance between the points 0.5 cm).

If you are using a wooden board then you should use nails to mark the points. So you should have at least 150 nails because some nails may break while hammering the nails. Carefully place each nail at the exact points.

Now the platform is ready for string art. Let's do string art.

3. To start with the string, select any adjacent sides of the triangle. Connect the string from the starting point of one side to the ending point of the adjacent side.

For example: take **AC** and **CB** as adjacent sides. Connect a string from point **C1** to **B1**. As shown in the figure.

Tie the tip of the string to the nail in the point **C1** and tightly connect the string to the nail in the point **B1**. No need to tie the string to the point **B1**, just wrap the string on the nail and continue to the next step.

Note: wrap the string on the nail whenever the direction of the string is changed.

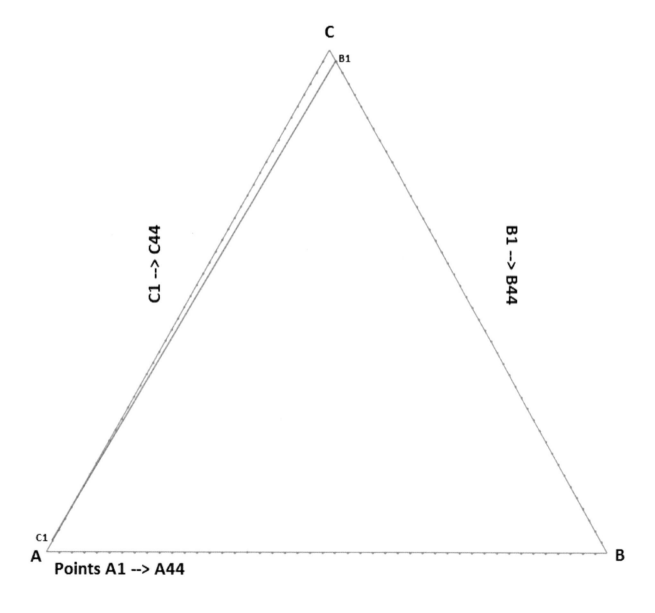

4.   Connect **B1** to **C2**, then **C2** to **B2** as shown in the figure.
After wrapping the string on the nail in **B1**, tightly connect the string on the nail at point **C2** then wrap the string on that nail. Then connect to the nail in the point **B2** then wrap on the nail. Continue to the next step.

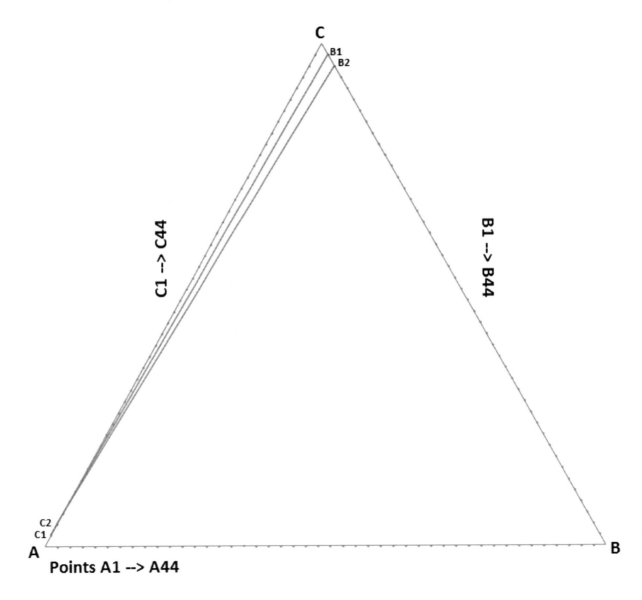

Points A1 --> A44

You can't really see the string connection to **C1** and **C2** points because the angle is very narrow.

But you can follow the steps mentioned to get the exact perfect result. Connect the string to the nail very tightly to get a perfect design pattern. This is the key and very basic step to do a perfect string art.

5. Continue these steps until you reach to get connected with the nails in the points **C44** to **B44**.

For Example: connections of the string after step 4 will be as follows: **B2** to **C3**, **C3** to **B3**, **B3** to **C4**, **C4** to **B5**, and so on.

At **B44** you need to tie the string because this will be the last point. Perfectly tie the string and Cut the remaining string. You will get the result as shown in the figure.

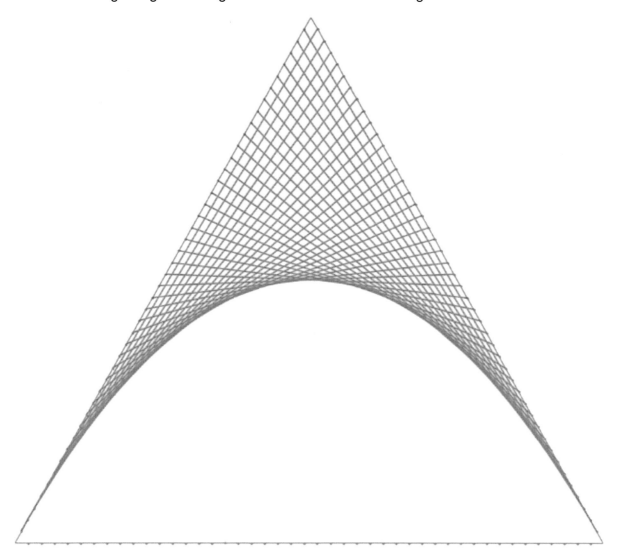

Note: This is the very basic step for most of the string art for any geometric shapes except round shape. We will see how to do the string art in round shape in the next design.

Proceed to the next steps to complete the triangle string art design.

6.   Same steps should be done for the other sides of the triangle as shown in the figure. Take the next adjacent sides as **CB** and **BA**. So that you will get the result as shown below.

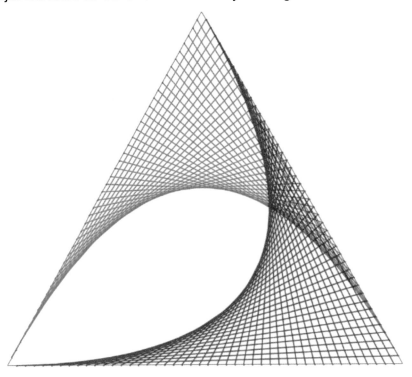

7.   After that do the same in the last adjacent sides **BA** and **AC**. You will get the final result as shown in the figure.

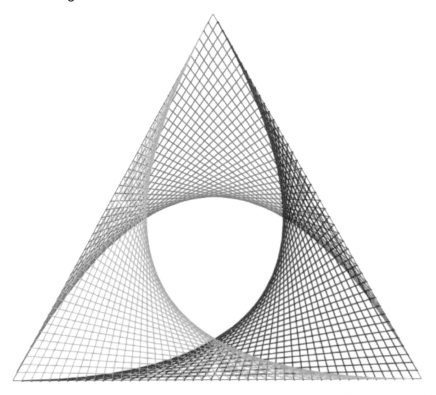

It is Very simple, easy and fun, isn't it? Let's do another one in round shape.

Note: I have also created a video for the same on YouTube for better understanding. You can see the video by clicking the link here: Triangle String Art

Please see below steps from start to end:

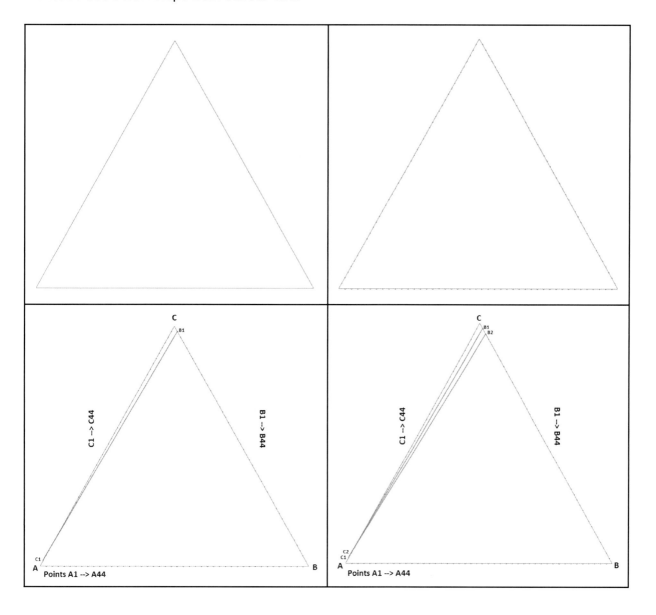

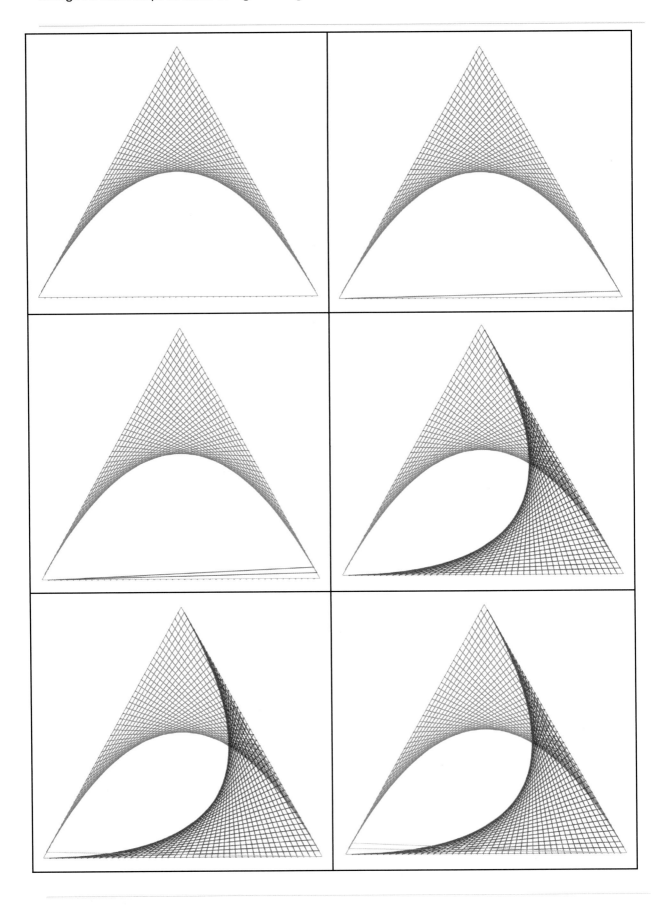

Final Result:

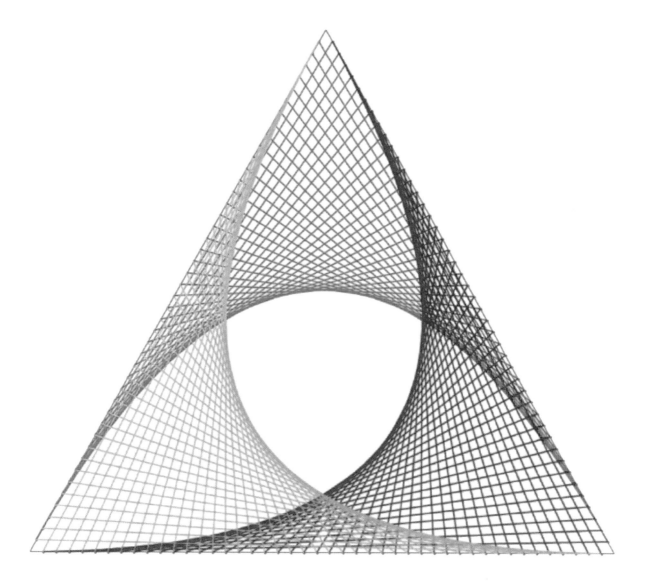

Video link: Triangle String Art

String Art Design: 2

Basic pattern: Round string Art

We are going to make the second basic String art as show in the below figure:

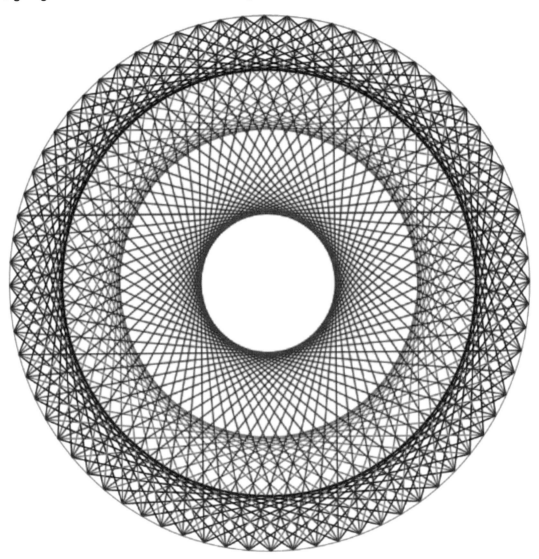

Materials used:

- Pencil, ruler, Compass
- 3 different colour strings (Blue, Green and Red). You can pick your own colours.
- Wooden board or Cardboard. You can pick your own platform like paper, thermocol, etc.
- Hammer and Nails (for wooden board).

Please follow the steps mentioned below to get a good result:

1. Draw a circle and divide the circle as shown in the figure. You should choose the radius of the circle according to the platform size.

For example: if the platform (Square) size is 30 cm in length, then the radius of the circle can be 12 cm to 13 cm.

Use the protractor to divide the circle. The total angle of the circle is 360 degrees. If the dividing angle is 5 degrees then you will get 72 points. The number of dividing points should be in the correct ratio for better results. You can decide the number of points you need on each side of the triangle. The perfect ratio will give a good result.

If you are using a wooden board then you should use nails to mark the points. So you should have at least 100 nails because some nails may break while hammering the nails. Carefully place each nail at the exact points.

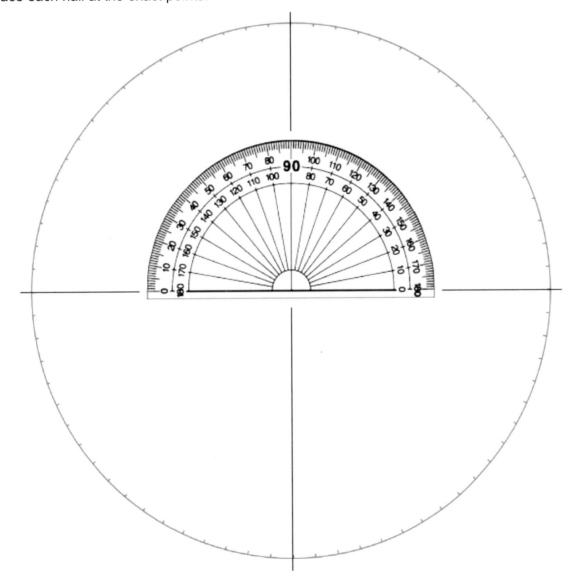

Now the platform is ready for string art. Let's do string art.

2.   Select a random point and tie the tip of the string to the nail in that point. Pick another point which is 10 to 15 points away from the first point, then connect the string to the second point.

For example: tie the string to the nail in the point **A1** then connect the string tightly to the nail in the point **A16** as shown in the figure. No need to tie the string to the nail at point **A16**, just wrap the string on the nail and continue to the next step.

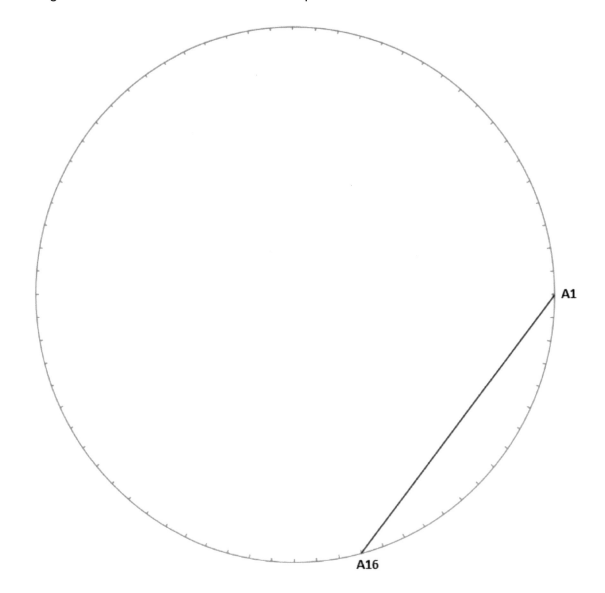

Note: Only need to tie the string at the first nail point. For all other nails, just wrap the string on the nail with the string.

3.   Connect the string tightly to the nail in the point **A2** from the point **A16**. Then **A2** to **A17** as shown in the figure.

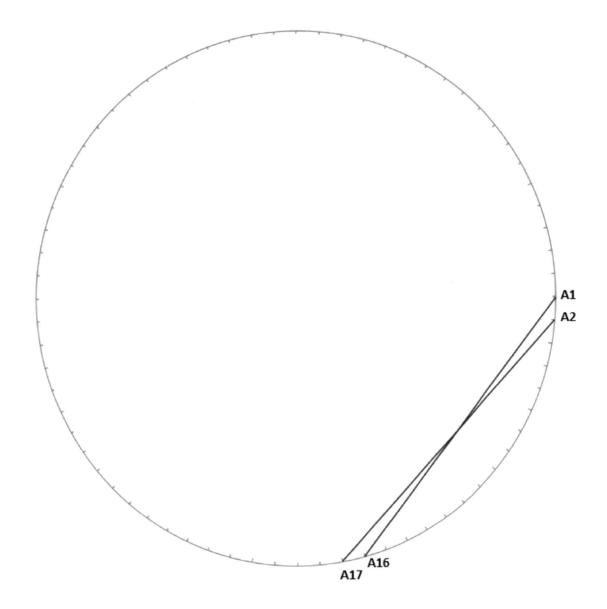

Note: This is the very basic step for most of the string art for round shape. Wrap the string on the nail whenever the direction of the string is changed. Connect the string to the nail very tightly to get a perfect design pattern. This is the key and very basic step to do a perfect string art. Make sure the string is very tight every time you connect the string from one nail to the other.

4. Repeat this process until you reach point **A1** again. Then tie the string to the nail in the point **A1**. You will get the result as shown in the figure.

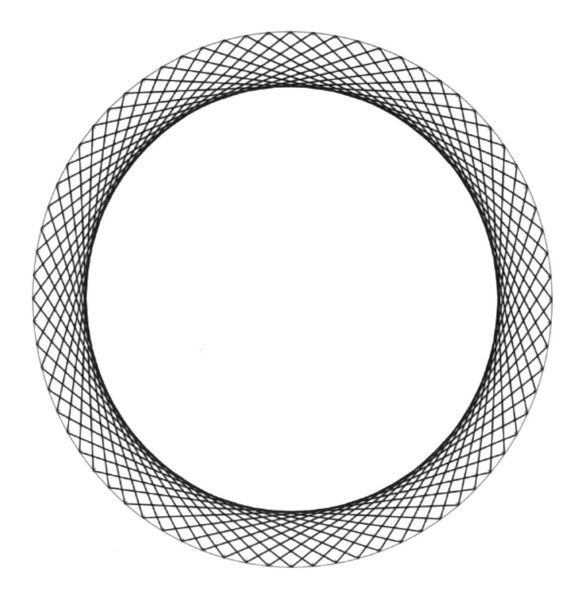

It is Very easy, isn't it? Let's continue to the next step.

5. Select a random point and tie the tip of the string to the nail in that point. Pick another point which is 20 to 25 points away from the first point, then connect the string to the second point.

For example: tie the string to the nail in the point **A1** then connect the string tightly to the nail in the point **A23** as shown in the figure. No need to tie the string to the nail at point **A23**, just wrap the string on the nail and continue to the next step.

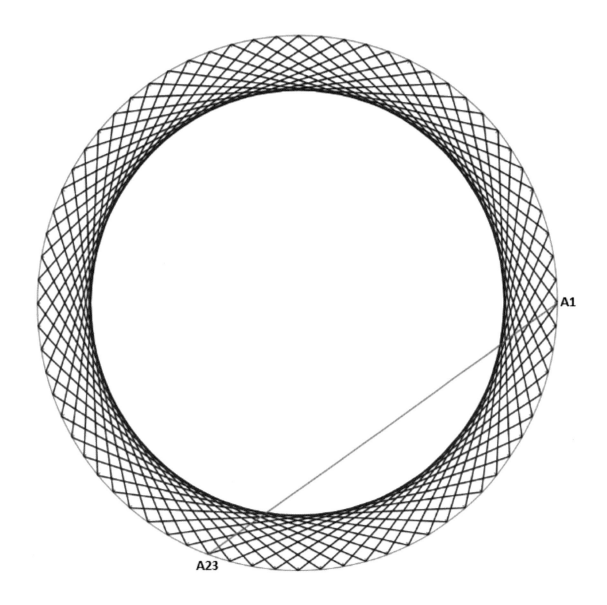

6. Connect the string tightly to the nail in the point **A2** from the point **A23**. Then **A2** to **A24**.

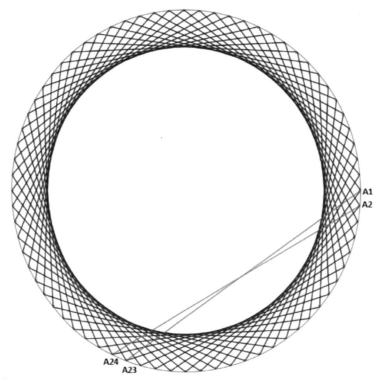

7. Repeat this process until you reach point **A1** again. Then tie the string to the nail in the point **A1**. You will get the result as shown in the figure.

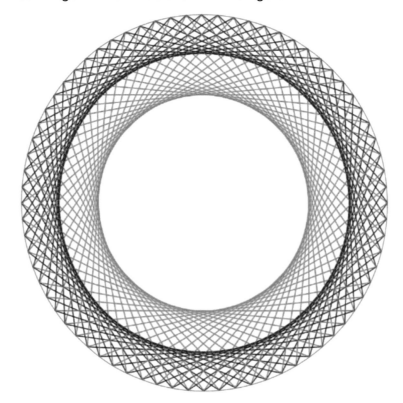

8. Continue to the final steps by selecting a random point and tie the tip of the string to the nail in that point. Pick another point which is 20 to 25 points away from the first point, then connect the string to the second point.

For example: tie the string to the nail in the point **A1** then connect the string tightly to the nail in the point **A31** as shown in the figure. No need to tie the string to the nail at point **A31**, just wrap the string on the nail and continue to the next step.

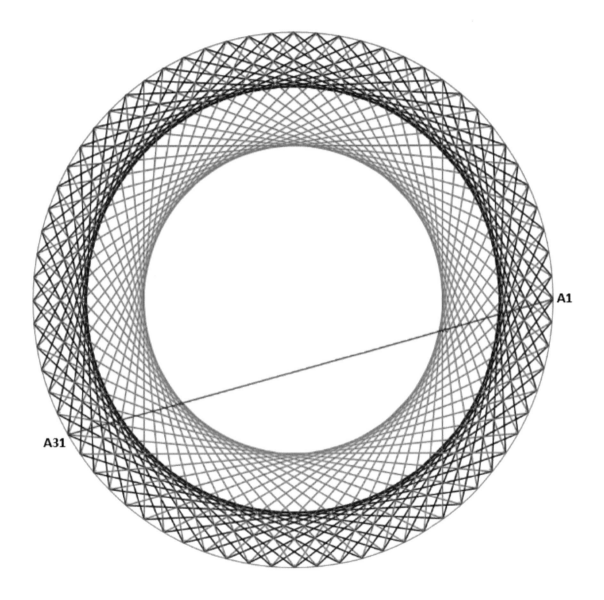

9. Repeat the same process we have done. You will get the final result as shown in the figure.

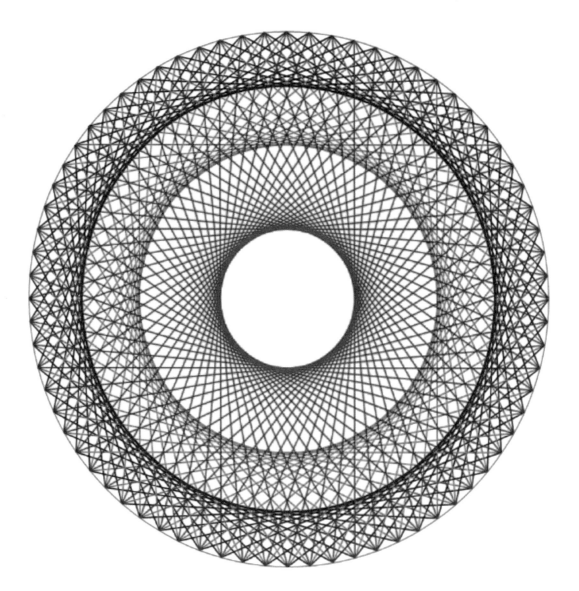

Note: I have also created a video for the same on YouTube for better understanding. You can see the video by clicking the link here: Round String Art

Please see below the steps from start to end:

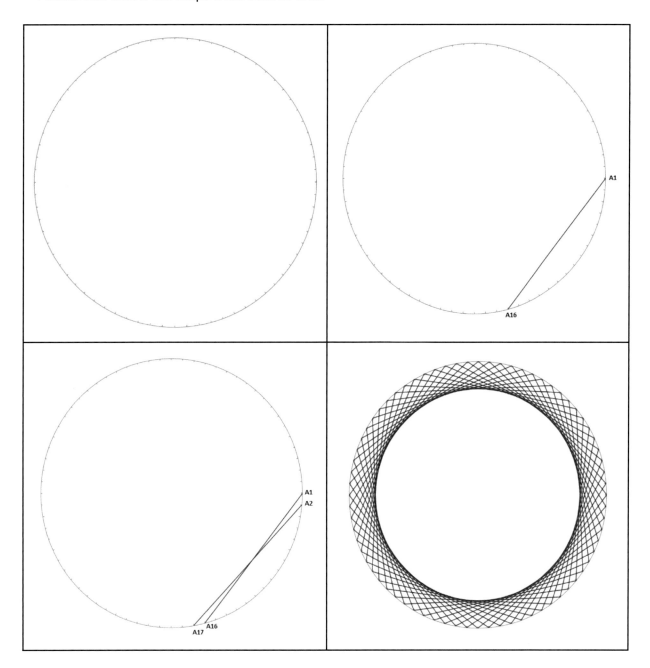

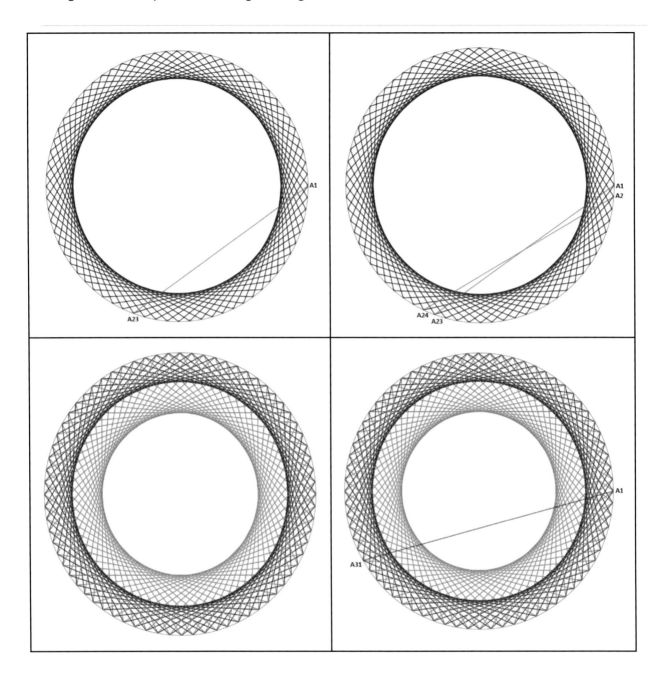

Final Result:

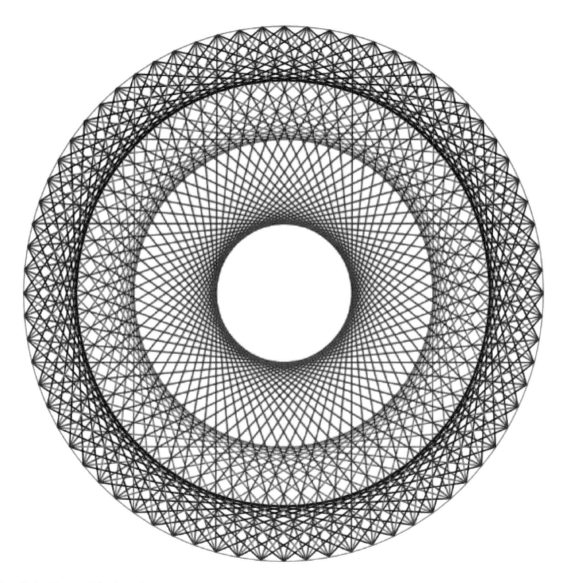

Video link: Round String Art

String Art Design: 3

Basic pattern: Triangle string Art

We are going to make the third basic String art design as show in the below figure:

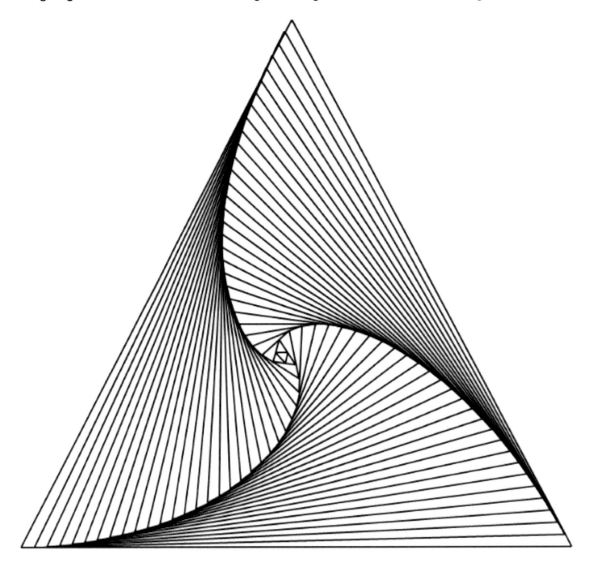

Materials used:

- ☐ Paper, Pencil and ruler.
- ☐ String. You can pick your own colour.
- ☐ Wooden board or Cardboard. You can pick your own platform like paper, thermocol, etc.
- ☐ Hammer and Nails (for wooden board).

Please follow the steps mentioned below to get a good result:

1. Draw a triangle with equal sides (Equilateral triangle). Length of the side should be according to the platform size.

For example: sides can be 20 cm if the platform size is 30cm (square shape). Draw the triangle with the sides of **AB=AC=BC**=20 cm. See the steps below to draw the equilateral triangle with 20cm side length.

    1.1.   Draw a line **AB** of 20cm using a pencil and ruler.

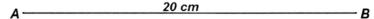

    1.2.   Take 20cm in the compass and mark arcs as shown in the figure from both points **A** and **B**.

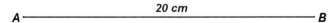

    1.3.   Draw lines from points **A** and **B** to the arc intersecting point **C**.

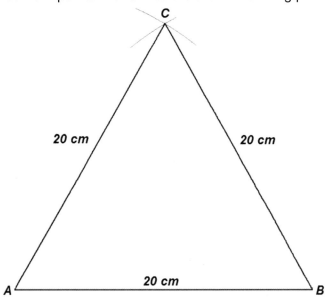

    1.4.   Now you have a triangle with 20cm each side.

For This string art design, it is better to draw the complete design first to get the points to make string art.

2. Mark a point **C1** 0.5 cm to 1 cm away from point **C**. You can choose the length of the distance according to the size of your own triangle. Mark another point **A1** 0.5 com to 1 cm away from point **A**. Draw a line from point **C1** to **A1** as shown in the figure.

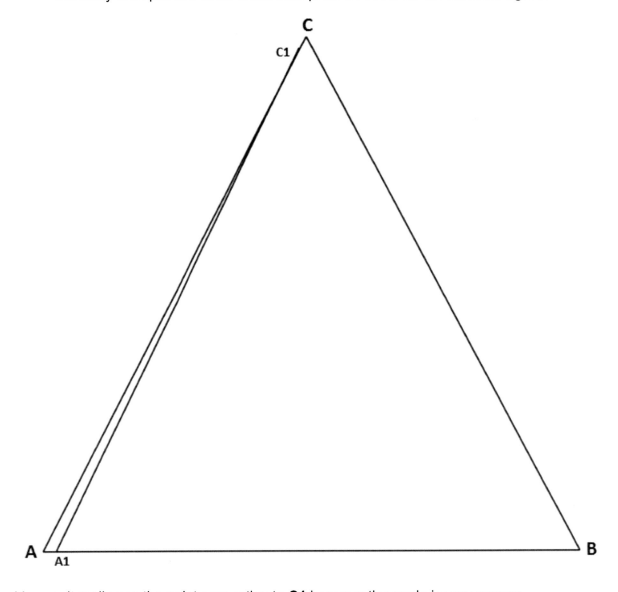

You can't really see the point connection to **C1** because the angle is very narrow.
But you can follow the steps mentioned to get the exact perfect result. In this example the point **C1** is 0.5 cm to 1 cm away from point **C**.

3. Mark another point **B1** 0.5 com to 1 cm away from point **B**. Draw a line from point **A1** to **B1** as shown in the figure.

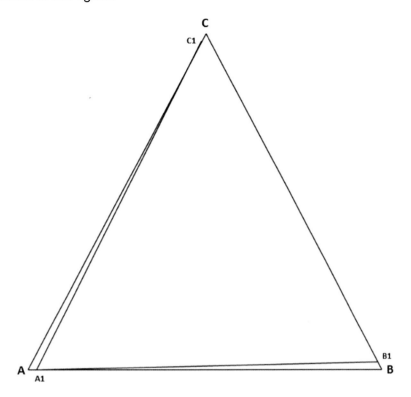

4. Connect the points **B1** and **C1**. You will get an inner triangle as shown in the figure.

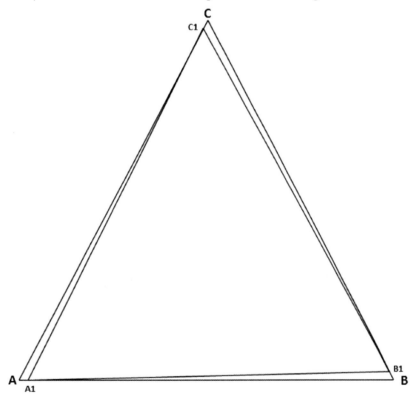

5. In the line **C1-A1**, mark a point **C2** 0.5 cm to 1cm away from point **C1**. Please note that, you should not mark this point **C2** on line **C-A**. You will not get this design if you mark the point **C2** in line **C-A**. You should mark it on line **C1-A1**. Like this mark point **A2** on line **A1-B1** and mark another point **B2** on the line **B1-C1**. Draw the line connecting the new points **C2**, **A2** and **B2**. You will get the result as shown in the figure.

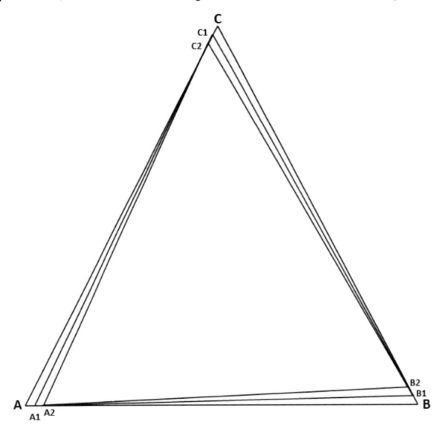

6. Repeat this process 10 -15 times, you will get the result as shown in the figure:

7.   Continue the same process until you reach the center to get the final result as shown in the figure:

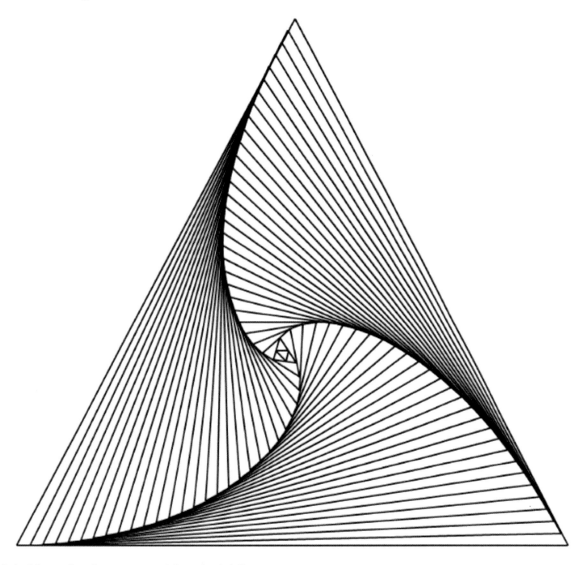

It is Very simple, easy and fun, isn't it?

Now you have the string art design in the paper. You can attach the design to the wooden board and place the nails in the points using a hammer. The platform will be ready after placing the nails in the exact position. Start connecting the points with a string exactly like we drew the lines connecting the points. You will get the final perfect result.

Optional: You can change the string colour after doing 5-10 rounds or 10-20 rounds as you wish.

Note: I have also created a video for the same on YouTube for better understanding. You can see the video by clicking the link here: Triangle String Art

Upcoming String art design projects

I have created some additional string art design for you. I'm sure you can try to make these designs with the knowledge from this book.

If you wish to get the step by step process for the following designs, let me know by adding the comments when you rate this book.

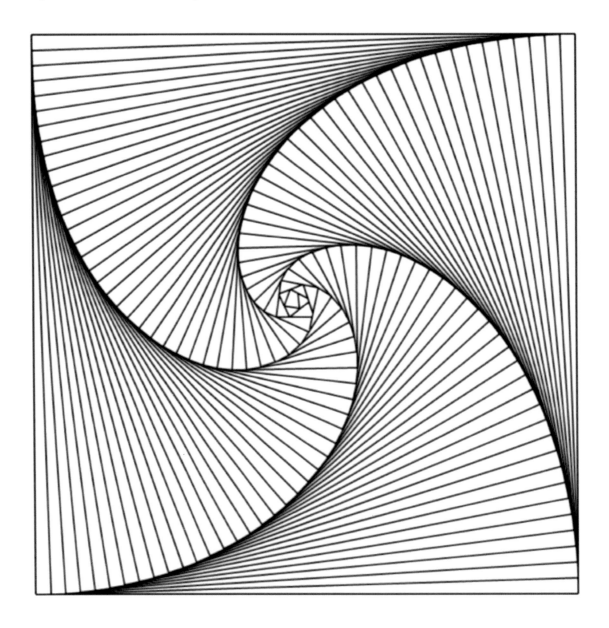

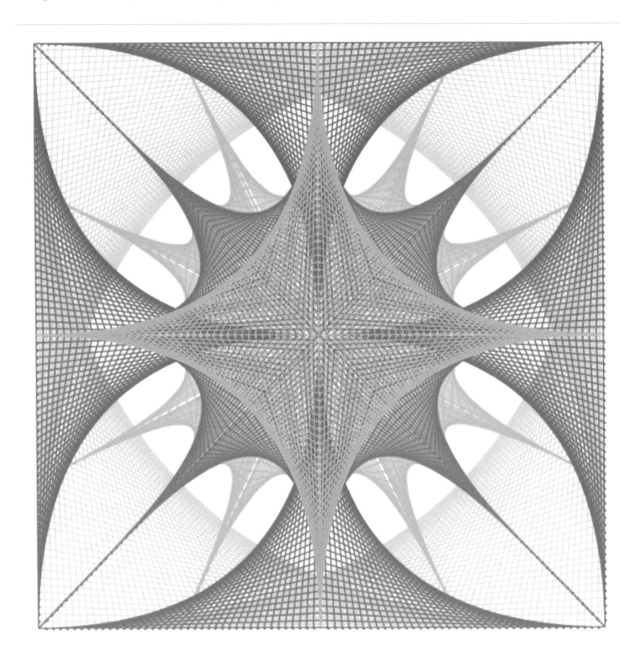